The Gift of Writing

by Kana Riley
illustrated by
Yvonne Buchanan

Scott Foresman

Editorial Offices: Glenview, Illinois • New York, New York
Sales Offices: Reading, Massachusetts • Duluth, Georgia
Glenview, Illinois • Carrollton, Texas • Menlo Park, California

Aunt Martha had a special gift.
She was a writer.

"I wish I could write like you,"
Abby said. "I never have any good
ideas though."

The
Wedding
BY
Martha
Chapman
Thayer

"First you must busy your hands and feet. Then open your eyes and ears," said Aunt Martha. "Then you write. Come with me."

Aunt Martha led Abby out of town. "You can start by picking these berries," she said.

"How will picking berries help me write?" Abby asked.

"You never know where ideas will come from," Aunt Martha said.

For a time they picked berries. Abby thought as the handles on the old pails squeaked. Maybe she could write about a wild horse.

Soon the pails were full.

"Come," said Aunt Martha. "We will visit Miss Elsie."

"But I want to write," Abby said.

"Quiet now. Walking is good thinking time," Aunt Martha said.

So Abby thought and thought. "Maybe I can write about a boy who is sad."

At the farm, Miss Elsie gave
Abby a feather. Abby could only
think about writing.

Then she and her aunt walked back home. Abby thought and thought some more. "A wild horse. Also a sad boy. I know! What if the boy finds the wild horse?"

Back home, Abby said, "May I write now?"

"Not yet. We must also cook the berries," said Aunt Martha.

"I hope cooking does not take too long," Abby said.

"Don't be in a hurry," said Aunt Martha. "Ideas need time to get stirred around in your head."

"Just one more step," Aunt Martha said. "This is how you strain the berries."

Abby watched the slow drip, drip, drip as the berry juice became ink. More ideas came to her. "The boy can get hurt. And the horse can save him," she said.

"Watch," said Aunt Martha. "I'll cut the feather. You can dip it in the ink. Are you ready to write?"

"Yes!" Abby said. "I see now. We picked berries. We walked to get a feather. We made ink for writing. We did much more than that though!"

"All the time we were getting ideas!" said Abby.

"That's right," said Aunt Martha. "I'm ready to write too."